**Name**

Color the capital letters.

# Jesus said, "Love one another."

John 15:12a

Match the big picture to the little picture of the same face.

# BIBLE

**Activity Book • Preschool**

purposeful design®
p u b l i c a t i o n s

Colorado Springs, Colorado

Purposeful Design Publications is the publishing division of the Association of Christian Schools International (ACSI) and is committed to the ministry of Christian school education, to enable Christian educators and schools worldwide to effectively prepare students for life. As the publisher of textbooks, trade books, and other educational resources within ACSI, Purposeful Design Publications strives to produce biblically sound materials that reflect Christian scholarship and stewardship and that address the identified needs of Christian schools around the world.

References to books, computer software, and other ancillary resources in this series are not endorsements by ACSI. These materials were selected to provide teachers with additional resources appropriate to the concepts being taught and to promote student understanding and enjoyment.

Unless otherwise identified, all Scripture quotations are taken from the New King James Version®. Copyright © 1982 by Thomas Nelson, Inc. Used by permission. All rights reserved.

Printed in the United States of America
19                    5 6 7

*Elementary Bible, preschool*
Purposeful Design Elementary Bible series
ISBN 978-1-58331-266-7 Student edition   Catalog # 100P1

Purposeful Design Publications
*A Division of ACSI*
PO Box 65130 • Colorado Springs, CO  80962-5130
Customer Service: 800-367-0798 • www.acsi.org

# Table of Contents

Draw a picture of yourself next to Jesus.

Draw Macy's picture. Color.

**Name**

Mark capital **G** and lowercase **g**.

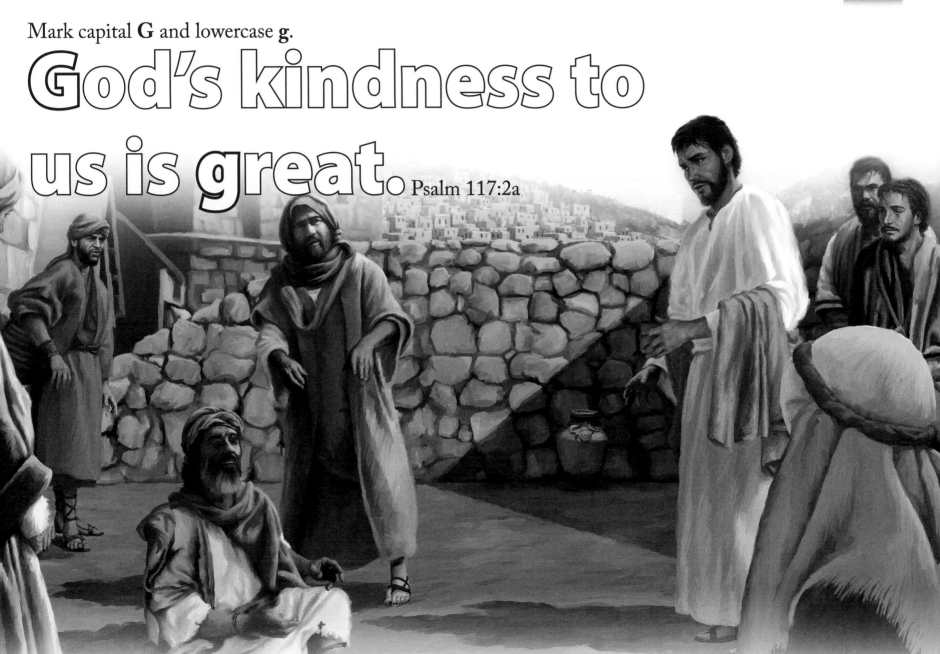

God's kindness to us is great. Psalm 117:2a

Match the pictures that feel the same.

**Name**

Trace the paths.

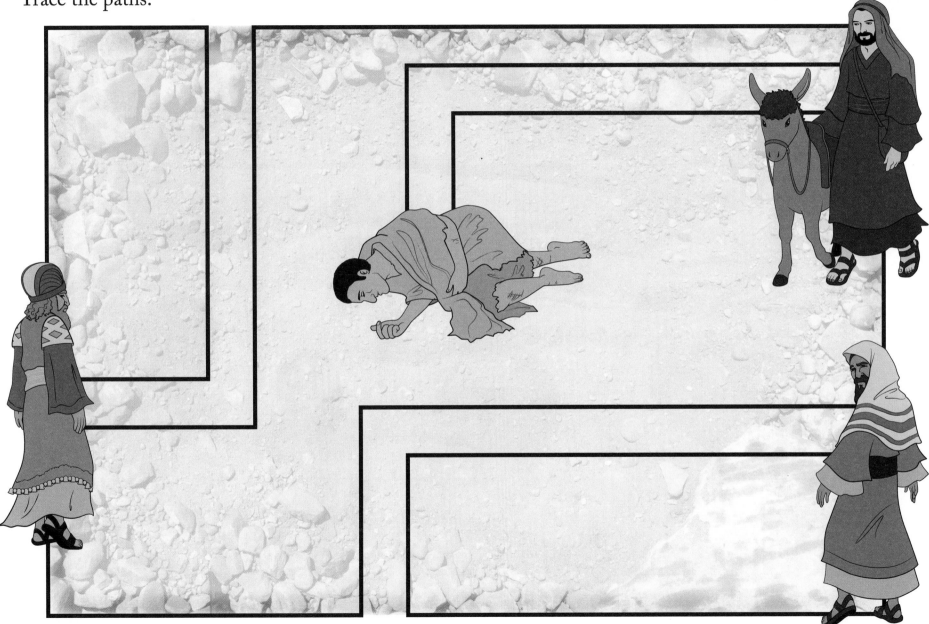

# Jesus Shows Kindness

John 9:1–38, Luke 10:25–37

Talk about the pictures.

Skill: expressive language/consideration

© Bible Preschool

Mark **e**.

Jesus said,
"I have come to give life."

John 10:10b

# Jairus' Daughter
Luke 8:40–56

Trace.

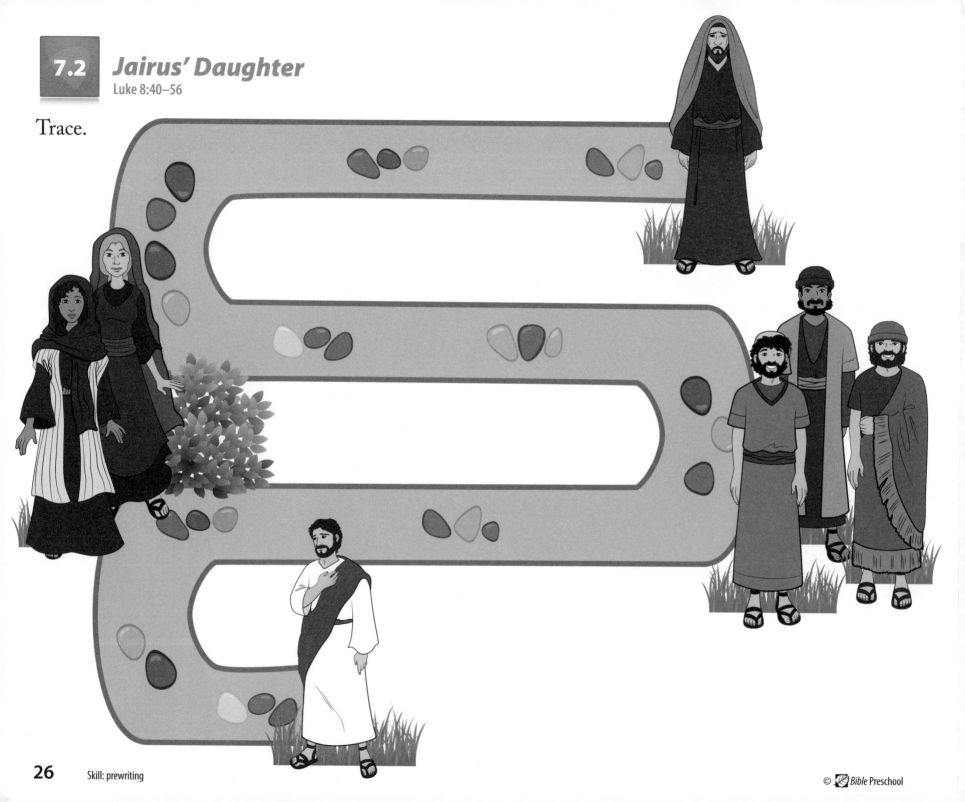

Skill: prewriting

© Bible Preschool

WHO CAN HELP US?

**1**

The girl said, "Mother, I feel sick. I can't play."

**3**

Then Jairus said to the mother, "Jesus loves little children. He can help us." Then he added, "I will go to Jesus. Only He can help us!"

**8**

"Thank you, Jesus! Thank you for helping us."

**6**

But the girl had died. The parents watched Jesus talk to her. He said, "Little girl, get up."

**2**

"I am sad," said the mother. "Our little girl can't run. She can't jump. She can't play. She is sick."
Jairus, the father, said, "I am sad. Who can help us?"

Jesus said, "Give food to her." The father said, "I am so happy. Thank you, Jesus!" The mother said, "I am so happy. Thank you, Jesus!"

**7**

**4**

"Where is Jesus?" said the father.
"There he is," said a man.

The father said, "Will you help us, Jesus? Our little girl is sick." Jesus said, "Yes, I will help you. I will come with you."

**5**

**Name**

Point to the letters you know.

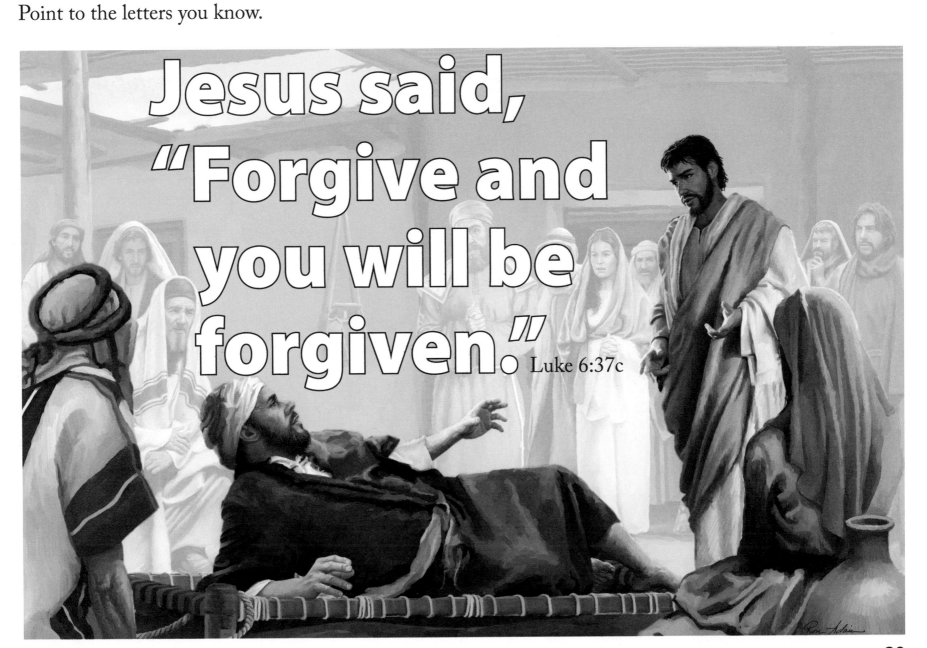

Jesus said, "Forgive and you will be forgiven." Luke 6:37c

Skill: letter recognition, visual discrimination

# Jesus Heals a Paralyzed Man

Mark 2:1–12, Luke 5:17–26

## Match the opposites.

stop

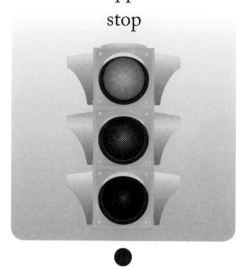

on

sick

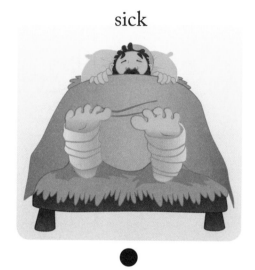

well

go

**Name**

**THANK YOU, GOD!**

**1**

**3**

He had some good friends. They believed that Jesus could heal their friend.

**8**

The man could walk! The people praised God! They had never seen anything like this miracle!

**6**

The friends climbed up on the roof. They made a hole in the roof. They helped the sick man go down into the room where Jesus was.

# Jesus Heals a Paralyzed Man

Mark 2:1–12, Luke 5:17–26

4

They made a mat for their friend. They carried him to the house where Jesus was.

2

There was a man who was paralyzed. He could not walk.

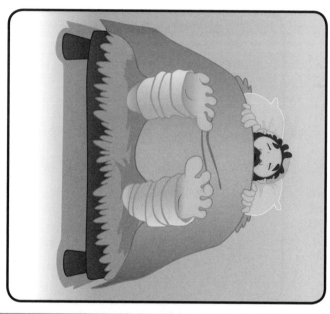

5

There were many people at the house. The men could not carry their friend through the door.

7

Jesus forgave the man for the sins he had done. Jesus healed the man. The man stood up. He picked up his mat.

© Bible Preschool

**Name**

Cut out the small pictures. Put each picture next to the twin it goes with.

Mark capital **T** and lowercase **t**.

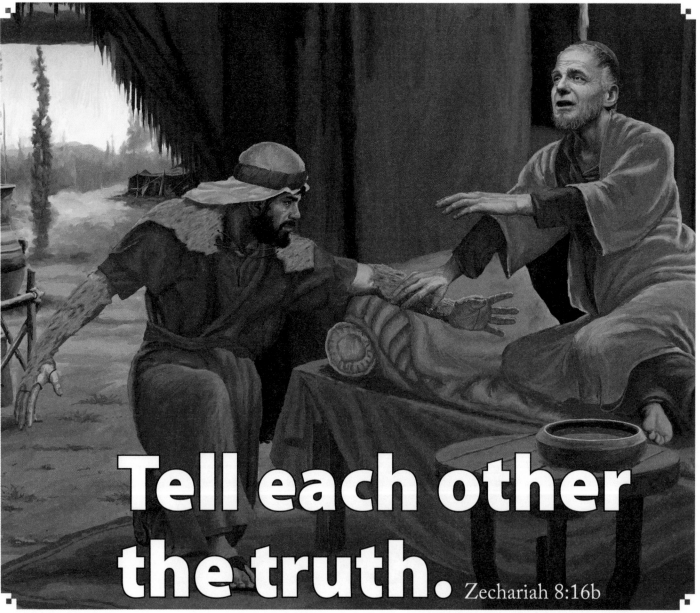

Tell each other the truth. Zechariah 8:16b

© Bible Preschool

Cut out the pictures to make a puzzle.

Talk about the pictures.

Name

Count the men. Color letter **o** in the Memory Verse.

Circle the thankful man.

Oh, give thanks to the Lord because He is good! 1 Chronicles 16:34a

Trace the path from the
thankful man to Jesus.

The 10 sick men called out to Jesus. They knew He could help.

2

Jesus healed the 10 men, but only one man turned back to thank Him.

4

## One Man Thanks Jesus

People were afraid of the 10 sick men. They did not want to get sick.

1

Jesus told the men to go to the temple. They were so happy!

3

TAPE BEHIND PAGE 2 OF *ONE MAN THANKS JESUS*.

1

We Thank and Praise God

I praise and thank Jesus when I pray to Him.

3

I praise and thank Jesus with my hands up high.

2

I praise and thank Jesus when I sing to Him.

4

I praise and thank Jesus for my food. I pray before I eat.

Color the letters in the word **God**.

With God nothing is impossible. Luke 1:37

Circle the picture of Joseph, Mary, or the angel that is different in each row.

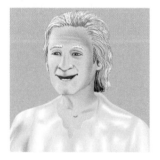   

**Name**

Take Mary and Joseph to Bethlehem.

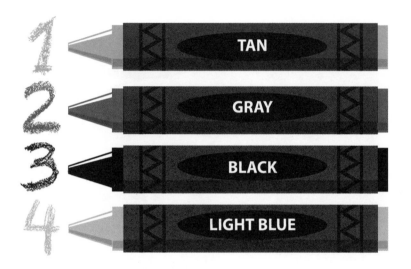

## 13.4 Mary and Joseph

Matthew 1:18–24, Luke 1:26–38, Luke 2:1–5

Color the picture by the numbers. Use the colors shown.

1 TAN
2 GRAY
3 BLACK
4 LIGHT BLUE

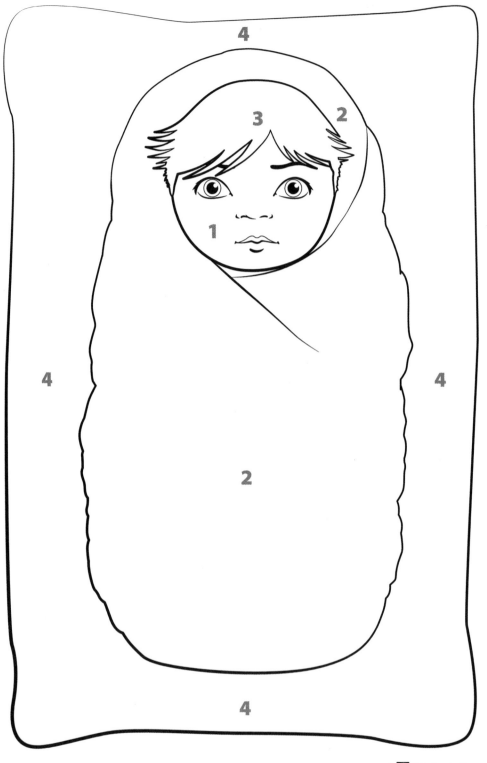

© Bible Preschool

Talk about the picture.

Today the Savior is born. He is Christ the Lord. Luke 2:11

Trace the gray lines to take each shepherd to Bethlehem.

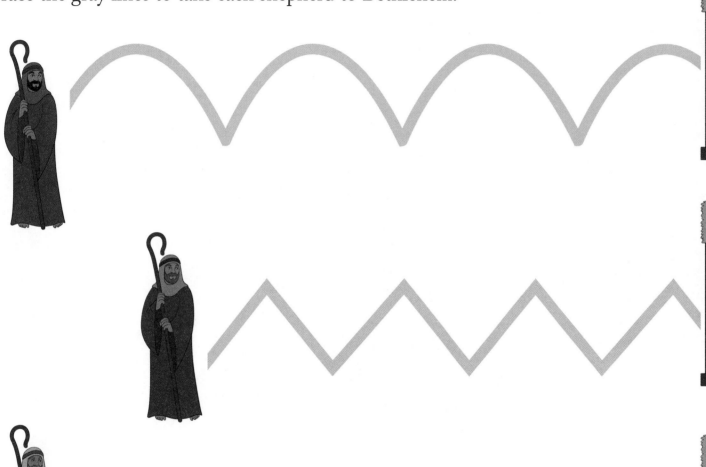

© *Bible* Preschool

**Name**

Cut out the small pictures. Glue them on the manger scene. Tell about the picture.

Find each small picture in the larger picture.

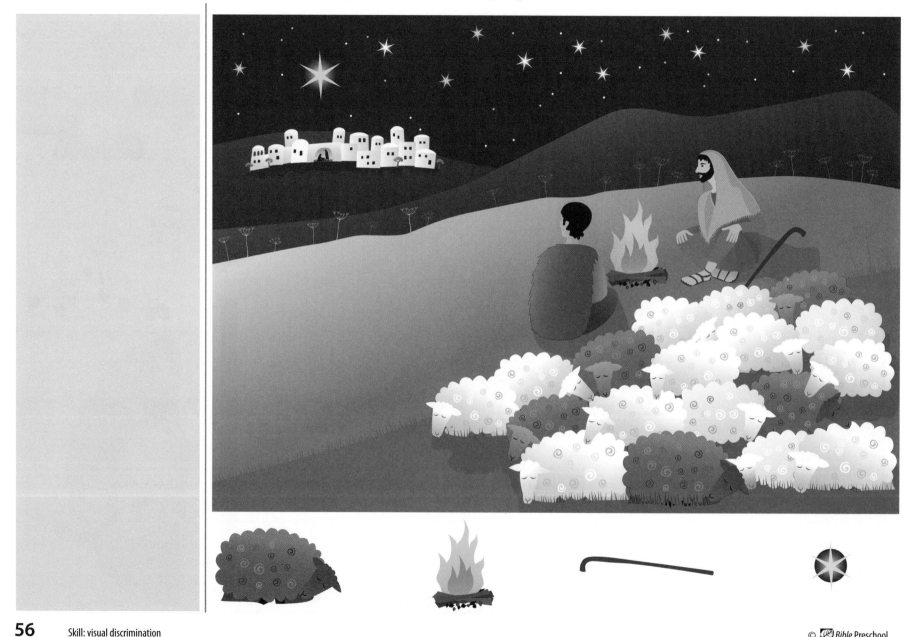

© Bible Preschool

Name

Talk about the picture. Mark the letter **s**.

We have seen His star and have come to worship Him. Matthew 2:2b

Count the yellow stars. Begin at each green star to trace the letters in **Jesus**.

Name

**Following the Star**

1

The wise men knew that this star meant that a new king was born. They packed their belongings and some gifts for the king.

3

God told the wise men not to go back to King Herod. They returned to their own country with great joy!

8

King Herod was angry! He wanted to be the only king. His helpers told him that the new king would be born in Bethlehem. So King Herod sent the wise men to Bethlehem.

6

**2** The wise men saw a bright, new star in the sky. This was a special star.

**4** When the wise men got to Israel, they went to King Herod's palace.

**5** The wise men asked King Herod where to find the new king.

**7** The wise men were so happy to see the star again! The star led them right to Jesus. They worshipped Jesus and gave Him gifts.

**Name** _____

Mark capital **M** and lowercase **m**.

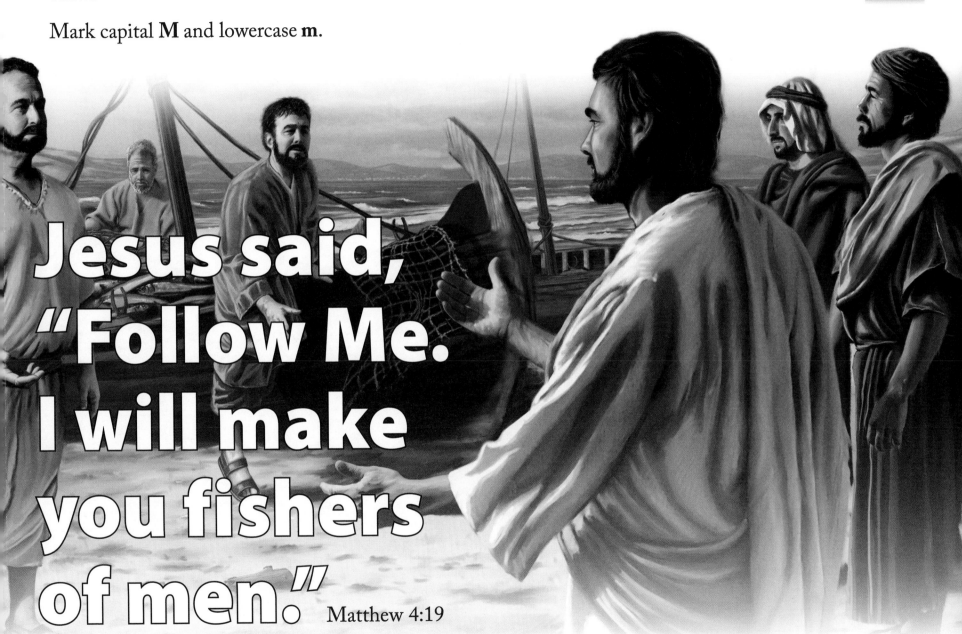

Jesus said, "Follow Me. I will make you fishers of men." Matthew 4:19

Count the fish in each group. Color the circle that tells the correct number.

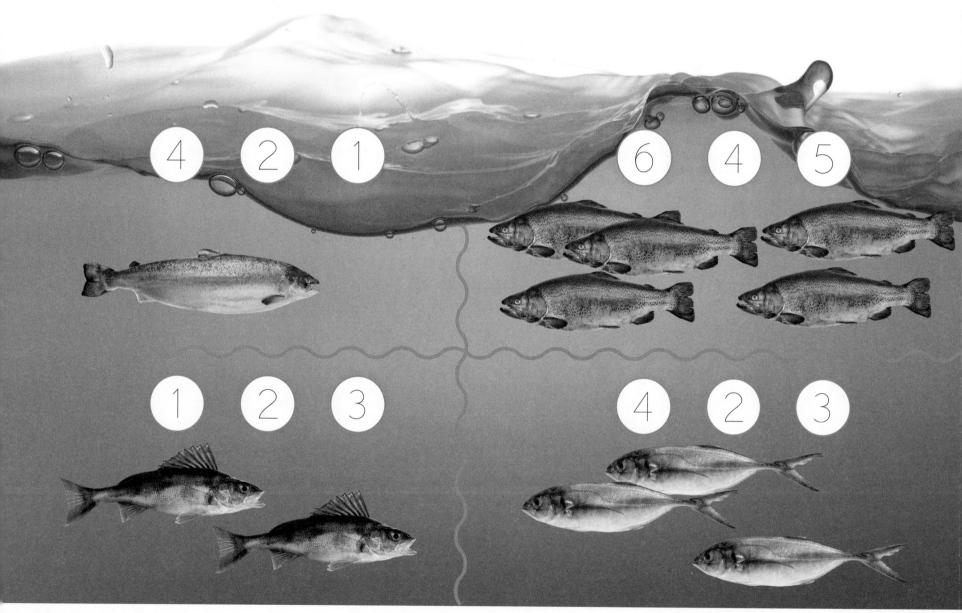

© Bible Preschool

Name

Matthew was collecting tax money when Jesus called him.
Can you find Matthew's missing coins? ⬭ Color them.

Talk about the pictures. How are the children being helpers?

© Bible Preschool

Mark lowercase **w.**

Even the wind and the waves obey Him. Matthew 8:27b

# Jesus Calms a Storm

Matthew 8:23–27, Mark 4:35–41, Luke 8:22–25

Cut out the small pictures. Put them in the large picture. Tell what is happening in the picture.

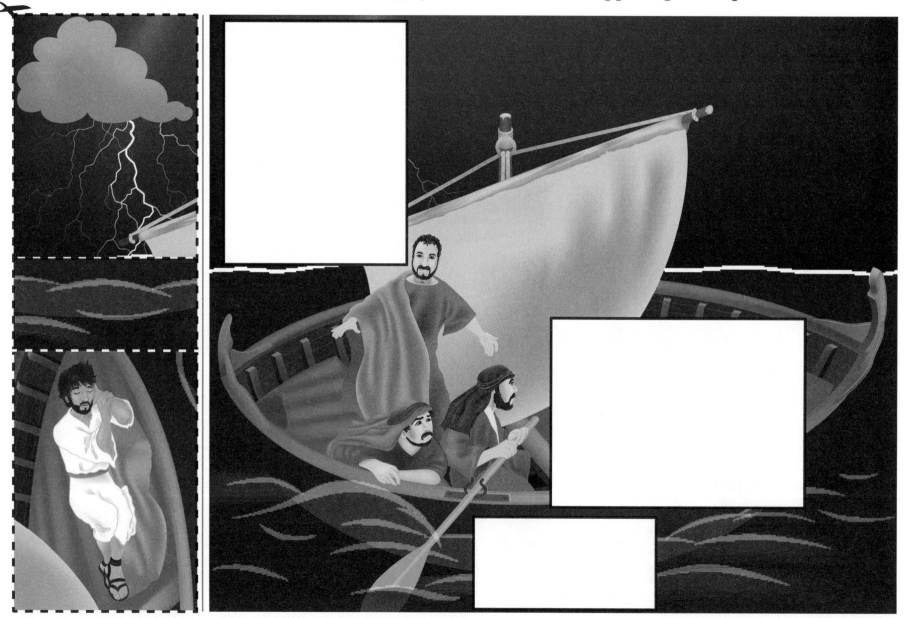

Skill: cutting, expressive language

© Bible Preschool

1

**GOD MADE THE WEATHER**

3

Sometimes it's hot.

Jesus is always near us.
He has power over the weather.

8

Sometimes it rains.
Everything gets wet!

6

# Jesus Calms a Storm

Matthew 8:23–27, Mark 4:35–41, Luke 8:22–25

4

Sometimes it's cold and snowy. We can make a snowman.

2

Sometimes it's bright and sunny.

Some days are cloudy and cool.

Sometimes the wind is very strong.

5

7

Skill: literacy

Color the letters you know.

# God loves a cheerful giver.

2 Corinthians 9:7b

# A Little Boy's Meal

John 6:1–13, Matthew 14:13–21

Find and mark:

2 ⬭

3 ◯

1 △

1 ♡

2 ◇

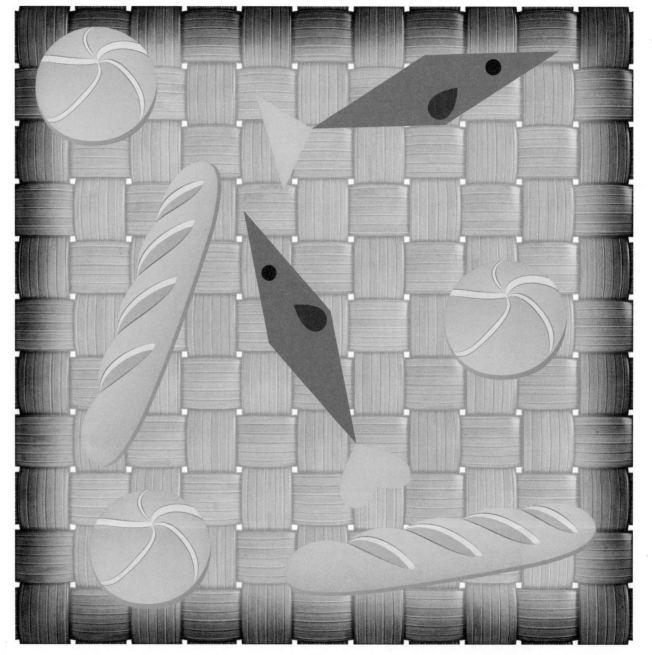

Skill: shape recognition, counting

© Bible Preschool

Name

## Jesus Feeds Crowds of People

1

Jesus taught many, many people. He knew that they were hungry, but there was no place to buy food.

2

One boy was willing to share his food. Andrew brought the boy to Jesus.

3

Jesus made the boy's little meal into a big meal for 5,000 people. Jesus did a miracle, all because the boy gave what he had to Jesus.

4

PLACE BEHIND PAGE 2 OF *JESUS FEEDS CROWDS OF PEOPLE*.

**1**

## We Like to Share

**3**

We share the tire swing.

**2**

We share the toys.

**4**

We share the paper. We all share God's love with others.

Mark the capital letters.

The disciples said, "You are the Son of God."

Matthew 14:33b

Color each area with **1** yellow. Color each area with **2** green.

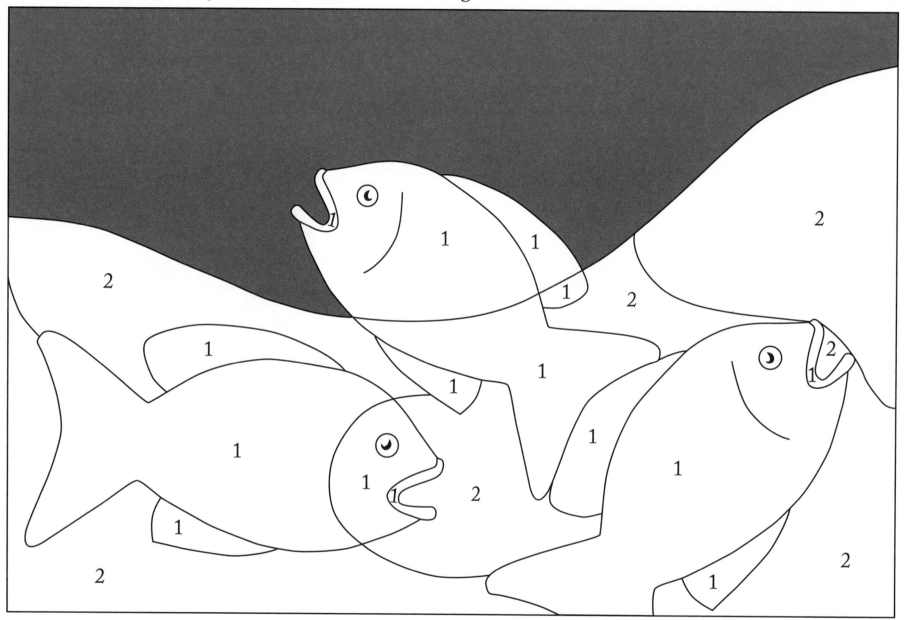

© Bible Preschool

**Name**

Take Jesus to Peter.

Talk about the pictures. Trace the letter **J**.

Jesus calms my fears.

**Name**

Mark the letter **o**. Circle the word **God**.

God keeps close watch on all my paths. Job 33:11b

Trace the gray lines to show who cared for baby Moses.

© Bible Preschool

**Name** _____

Find each small picture in the larger picture.

Look at each picture. Circle the person who is keeping the child safe.

Name

Look at the pictures. Tell how the children are working together.

Find and circle Moses, sandals, a fiery bush, and Moses' walking stick. Mark the letter **o** in the Memory Verse.

Do good to all people.
Galatians 6:10b

© Bible Preschool

Name

Count the flies, grasshoppers, and frogs. Circle or mark the box that tells the correct number.

1 4 8

3 2 4

4 6 7

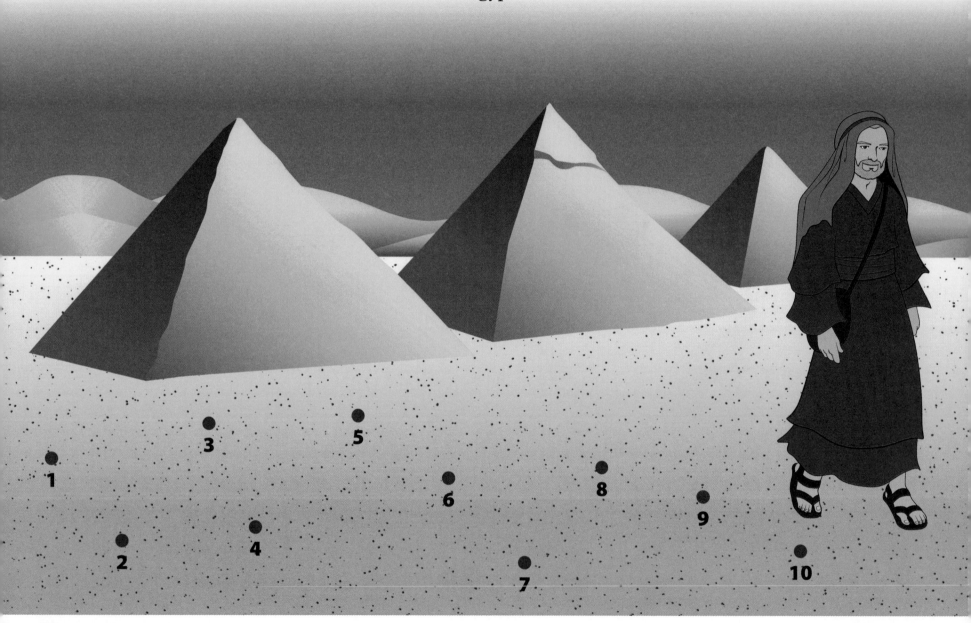

Connect the numbers 1–10 to follow Moses out of Egypt.

© Bible Preschool

**Name**

Color capital **S**.

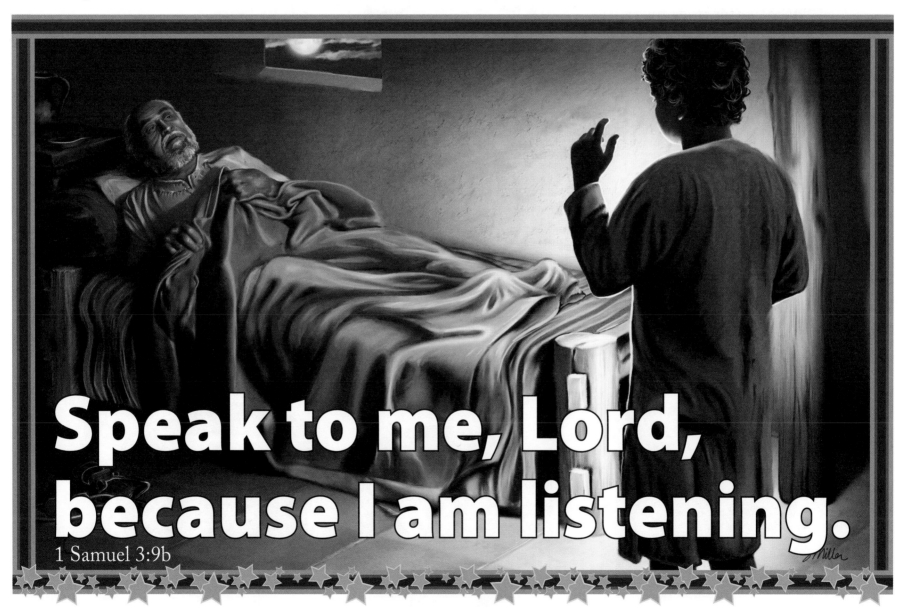

Speak to me, Lord, because I am listening.

1 Samuel 3:9b

## 22.2 Young Samuel

1 Samuel 3:1–20

Find Samuel.
What letter does his name begin with? What other words begin with **s**? Draw a line from the words that begin with **s** to the capital letter **S**.

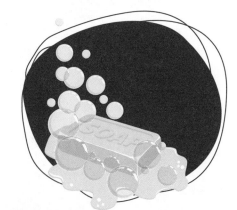

Skill: letter recognition, initial consonant sound

© Bible Preschool

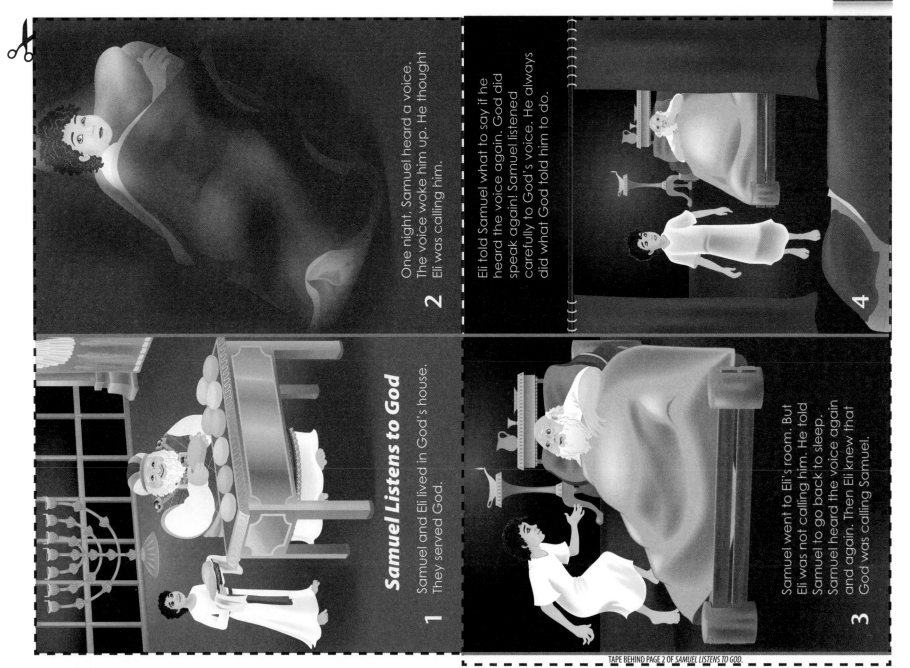

**Samuel Listens to God**

**1** Samuel and Eli lived in God's house. They served God.

**2** One night, Samuel heard a voice. The voice woke him up. He thought Eli was calling him.

**3** Samuel went to Eli's room. But Eli was not calling him. He told Samuel to go back to sleep. Samuel heard the voice again and again. Then Eli knew that God was calling Samuel.

**4** Eli told Samuel what to say if he heard the voice again. God did speak again! Samuel listened carefully to God's voice. He always did what God told him to do.

TAPE BEHIND PAGE 2 OF *SAMUEL LISTENS TO GOD*.

1 Sssh! Listen!

2 I like to listen to music.

3 I like to listen to whispers.

4 I like to listen to stories from God's Word.

**Name**

Trace the path to take the sheep to green grass. Stay away from the lion and bear!

Count David's brothers. Mark the word **heart**.

Trust in the Lord with all your heart. Proverbs 3:5a

Skill: counting, sight word recognition

**Name**

Trace the stones. Color five stones for David's slingshot.

Talk about the pictures.

© *Bible* Preschool

**Name**

Say the Memory Verse. Color the leaves that have the words of the Memory Verse.

Luke 19:10

Match the opposites.

happy

down

tall

up

short

sad

Skill: matching, expressive language

© *Bible* Preschool

**Name**

He saw the hills.
He saw the people.
He saw Jesus!

6

What a happy day
for Zacchaeus! Jesus knew
his name! Jesus loved and
forgave Zacchaeus.

8

Zacchaeus was very short. He could not
see over the crowd of people.

3

**ZACCHAEUS IS FORGIVEN**

1

Zacchaeus was a rich tax collector, but he wasn't happy. He wanted to see Jesus.

What could Zacchaeus do? Looking around, he noticed a sycamore tree.

Zacchaeus climbed higher and higher. Up! Up! Up!

"Zacchaeus, come down. I want to stay at your house today," Jesus said.

24.4 **Zacchaeus**
Luke 19:1-10

Put stars in the sky. Mark the letter **v**.

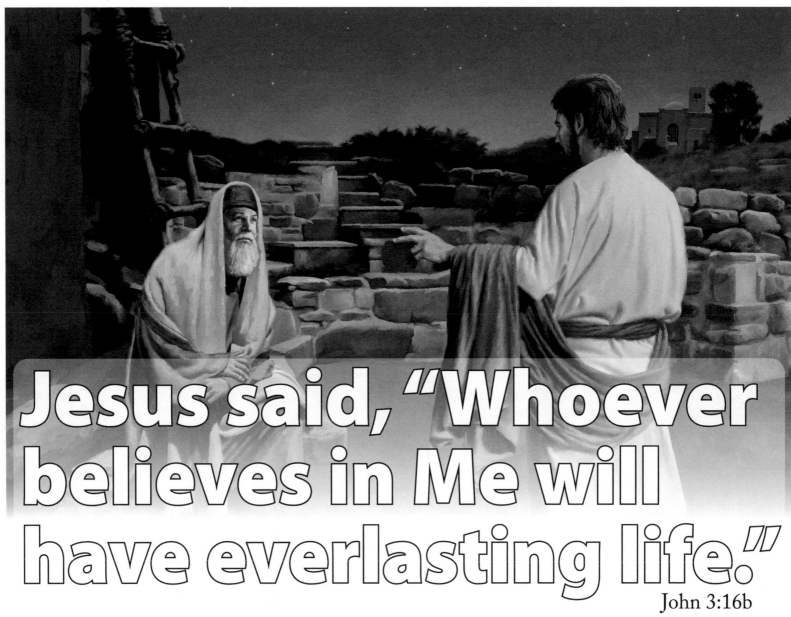

Jesus said, "Whoever believes in Me will have everlasting life."

John 3:16b

Skill: letter recognition

Match the pictures to the right time of day. Tell what the children are doing.

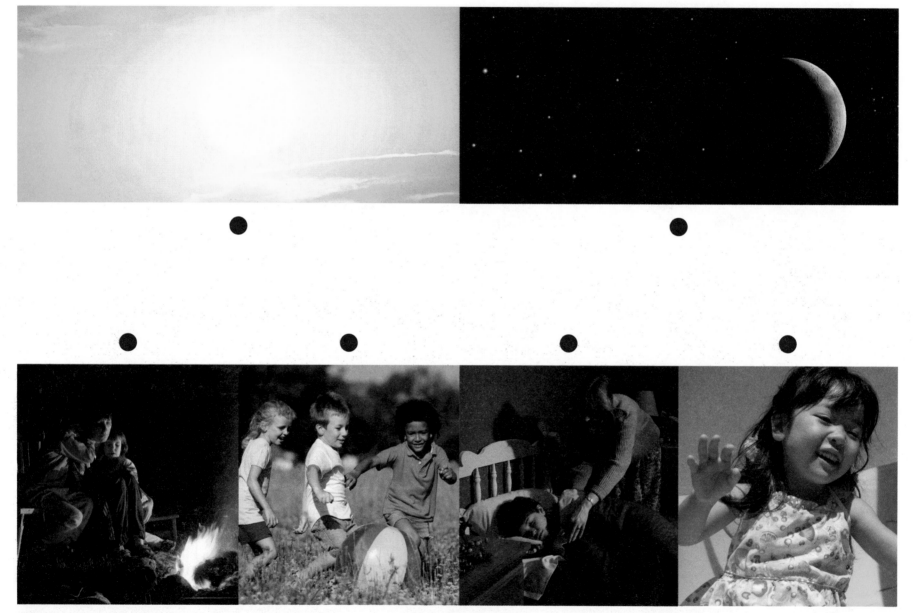

Skill: matching, expressive language

© Bible Preschool

**Name**

Color the hearts, cross, and world.

God loved the world so much

that He gave His only Son.

Skill: prewriting **99**

Nicodemus is happy because he believes in Jesus. Color Nicodemus according to the numbers.

1 TAN
2 GRAY
3 BLUE
4 LIGHT BLUE
5 BROWN

Count the food. Match the food with the correct number.

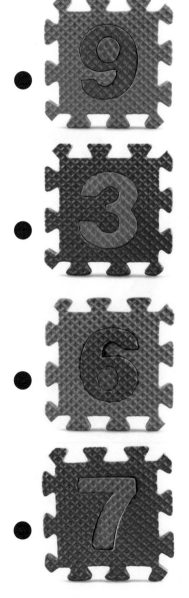

Say the Memory Verse. Color the stained-glass panels that have the words of the verse and its reference.

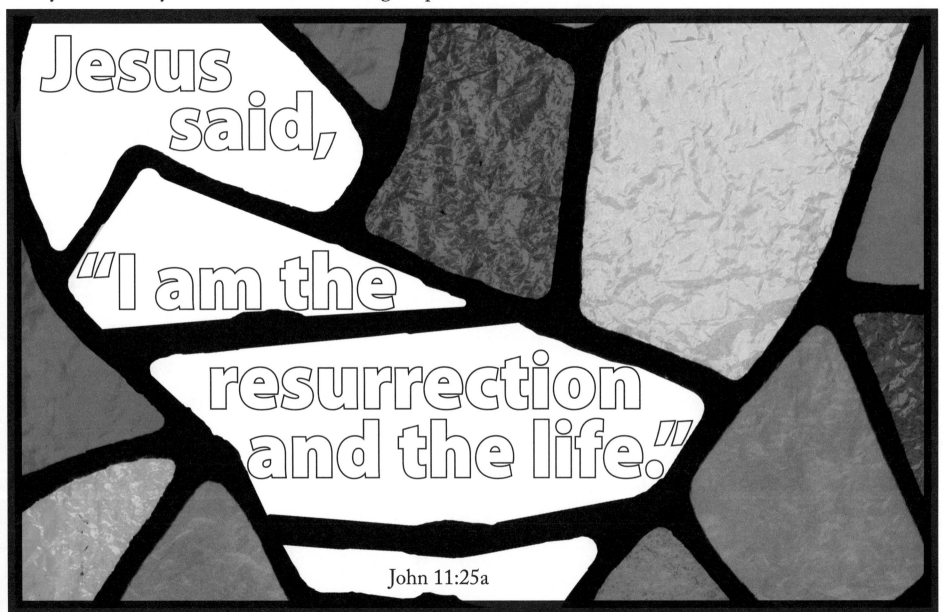

Jesus said, "I am the resurrection and the life."

John 11:25a

Listen to the poem. Talk about the pictures.

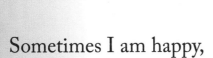
My Feelings

Sometimes I am happy,

Sometimes I am sad,

Sometimes I am silly,

Sometimes I am mad.

But no matter how I feel each day,
Jesus loves me anyway!

Cut out the rock and attach it over Lazarus. Lift up the rock to show that Lazarus is alive!

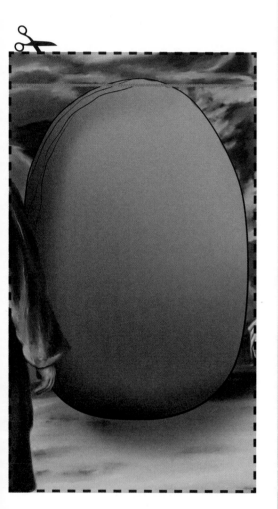

GLUE HERE

Skill: fine motor skills, expressive language

© Bible Preschool

Name _____

Circle capital **H** and lowercase **h**.

The people shouted, "Hosanna in the highest!"

Matthew 21:9a, d

# Jesus Enters Jerusalem
Matthew 21:1–11, 15–16; 26: 17–30

Everyone can praise God. How do you praise God? Talk about the pictures.

Jesus shared His last supper with His friends. Match the pictures that are alike.

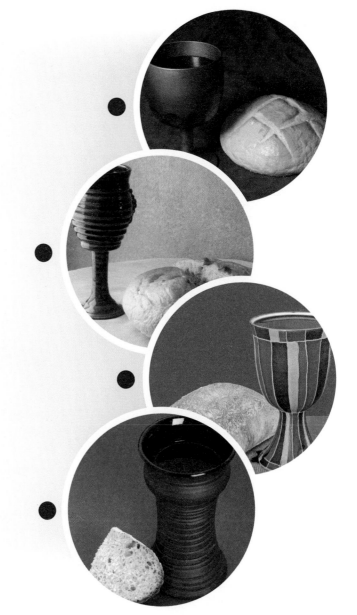

Draw your family sharing a meal.

Mark **i**.

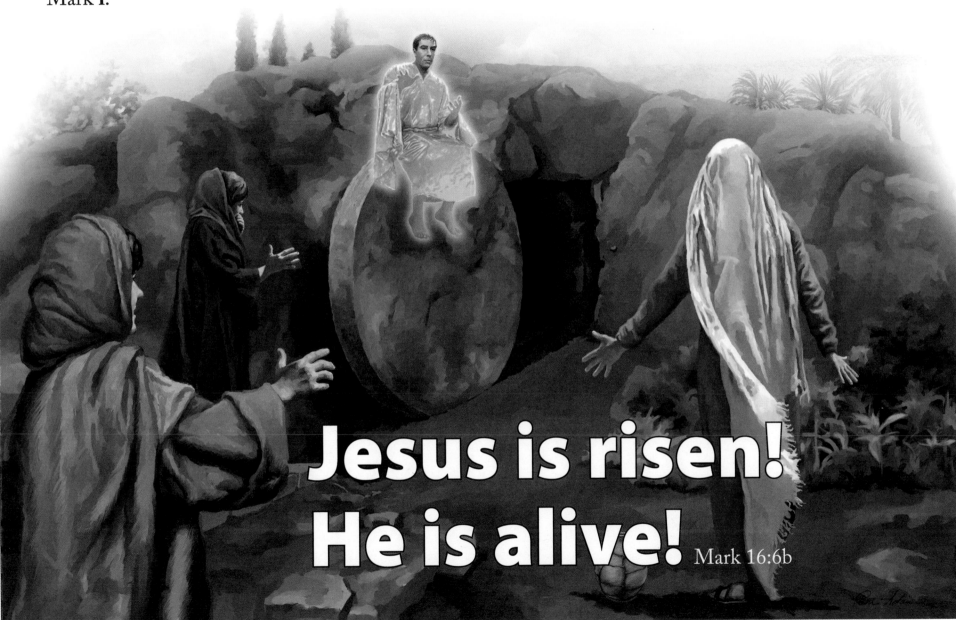

Jesus is risen! He is alive! Mark 16:6b

Add wings to the butterfly. Tell why the butterfly reminds you of Jesus.

Name

Take Jesus and His friends to Emmaus. Draw a path though each capital **E** and lowercase **e**.

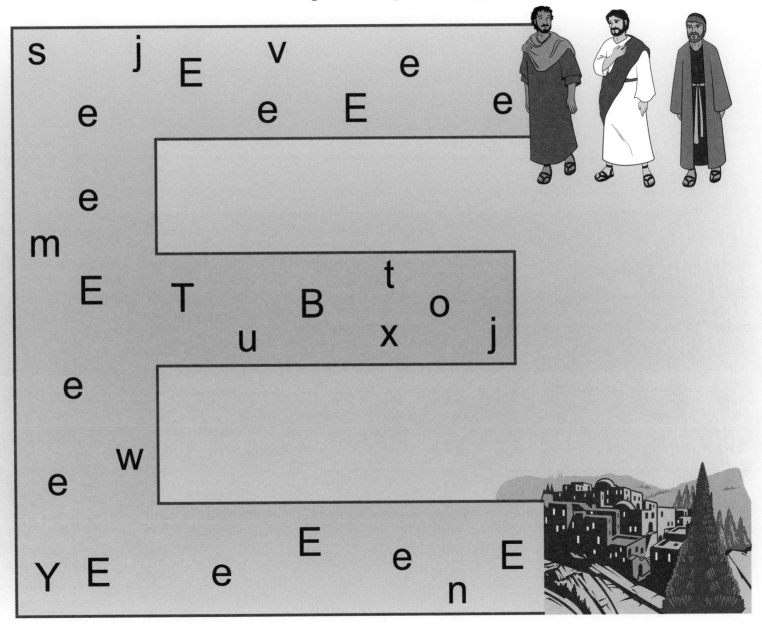

Add cotton to the clouds. Tell about the picture.

© Bible Preschool

Trace the word **God**.

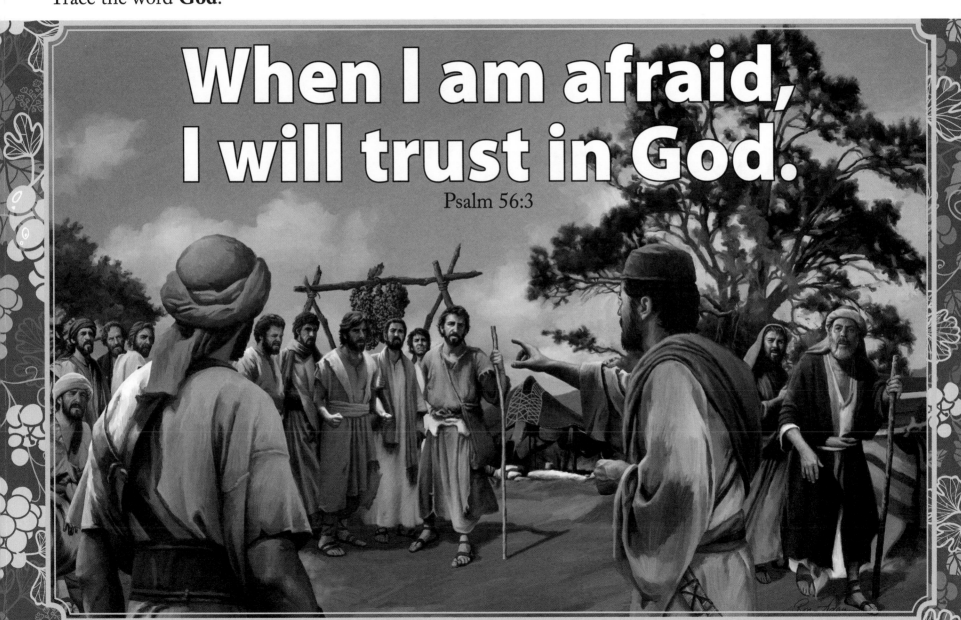

When I am afraid,
I will trust in God.
Psalm 56:3

Circle the two spies who trusted God. Cross out the 10 spies who did not trust God.

© Bible Preschool

Count the grapes. Mark the correct number.

Talk about the pictures. How is each child showing trust? Mark the picture you like the best.

© Bible Preschool

Name

The Israelites would soon have a new home. Match the homes.

Color the letter **e**.

The people said, "We will serve and obey God." Joshua 24:24

© Bible Preschool

**Name**

Count the horns. Trace the correct number.

5    6    7

Which cookies were baked according to the recipe? Make a line from those cookies to the bakers.

© Bible Preschool

**Name**

Find the small shapes on the larger picture. Draw a den for the lion.

Mark the letter **l**. Circle the word **God**.

# For He is the living God and He lives forever.
Daniel 6:26b

Skill: visual discrimination, letter recognition, sight word recognition

© *Bible* Preschool

Name

Cut out the pictures. Put them in order.

Make a puzzle.

**Name**

Say the rhymes. Cut out the pictures. Place each picture in the correct place. ✂

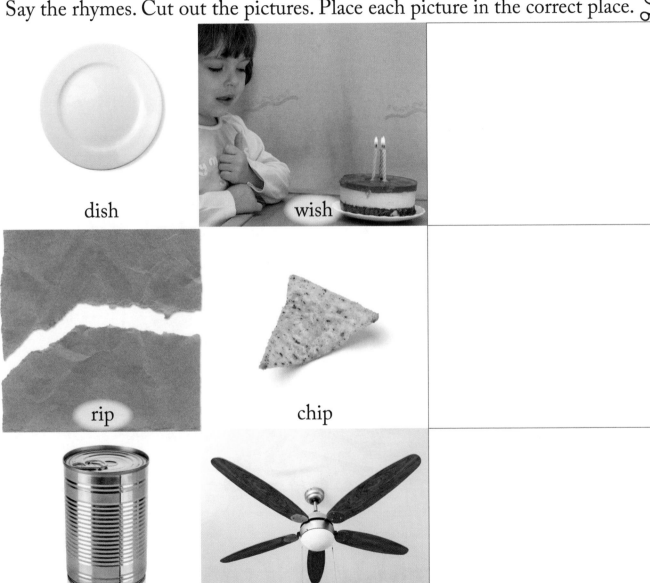

dish

wish

rip

chip

can

fan

ran

ship

fish

Mark the letter **d**.

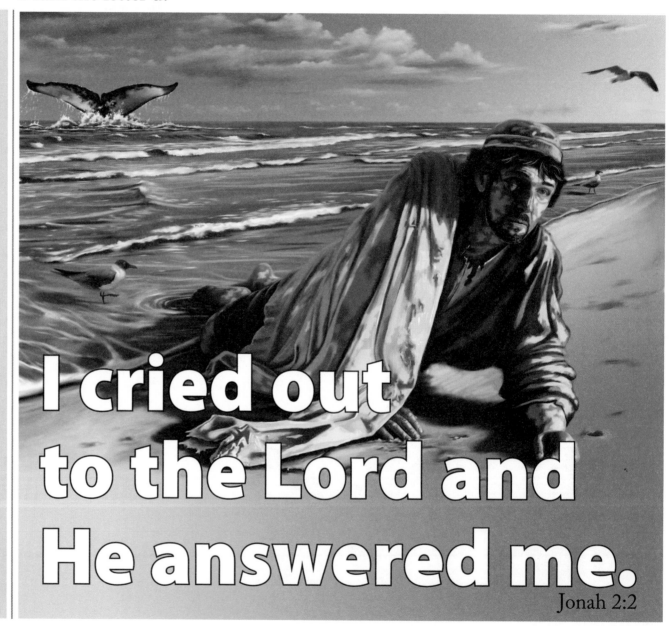

I cried out to the Lord and He answered me.

Jonah 2:2

Jonah
Runs
from
God

The prophet Jonah
would not obey.
He hid on a ship
and sailed away.

1

To Jonah's God the sailors did pray.
Then they tossed him into the ocean spray.

3

With thankful hearts the people began to pray,
"Thank you, God, for sending Jonah our way!

8

From deep in the belly, Jonah heard a sound.
Oh! That fish thew Jonah up on dry ground!

6

Skill: literacy    **127**

God sent a storm with waves that crashed. "Throw me in the ocean," said Jonah, "or we won't last!"

Down, down, down, down Jonah fell.

But God sent a great fish to keep him safe and well.

As fast as he could Jonah hurried away. God's message to Nineveh, he didn't delay.

For three days and nights Jonah prayed. "Oh, Lord, I'm sorry, I should have obeyed!"

Name

Mark capital **H** and lowercase **h**.

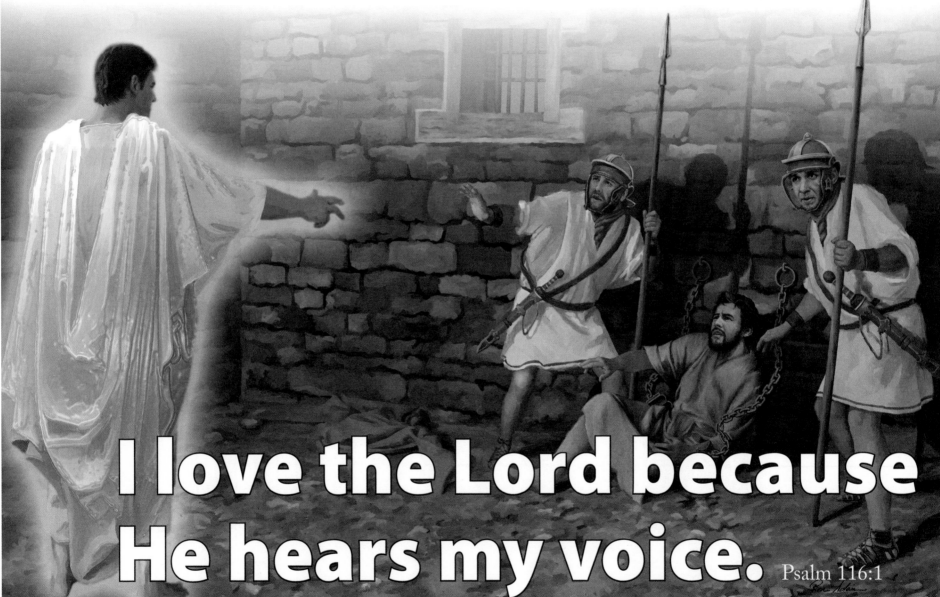

I love the Lord because He hears my voice. Psalm 116:1

Mark the letter that stands for the first sound in each picture.

**S  P  T**

**G  H  P**

**D  S  T**

**P  T  G**

© *Bible* Preschool

Name

Use the words in the box to read the story.

KEY

After Jesus went to heaven,  told many people about God's

plan to save all people who believe in Jesus as their Savior. Soon there

were many, many . Every day,  preached

about Jesus, but King Herod did not like that. He put  into

. Peter's friends were sad. They knew that the king would not

let  out of , so they .

 Peter

 believers

 prison

 angel

 knocked

 prayed

Use the words in the box to read the story.

Peter was in  when God sent an . The angel

told  to wake up. Peter's chains fell off. Peter followed the

angel out of the prison and past the iron gate. He went to Mary's house

and  on her door. He  and !

A little girl named Rhoda told the friends that Peter was there. All the

 were so happy to see Peter. God had answered their prayers.

**KEY**

 Peter

 believers

 prison

 angel

 knocked

prayed

Mark the letter **p**.

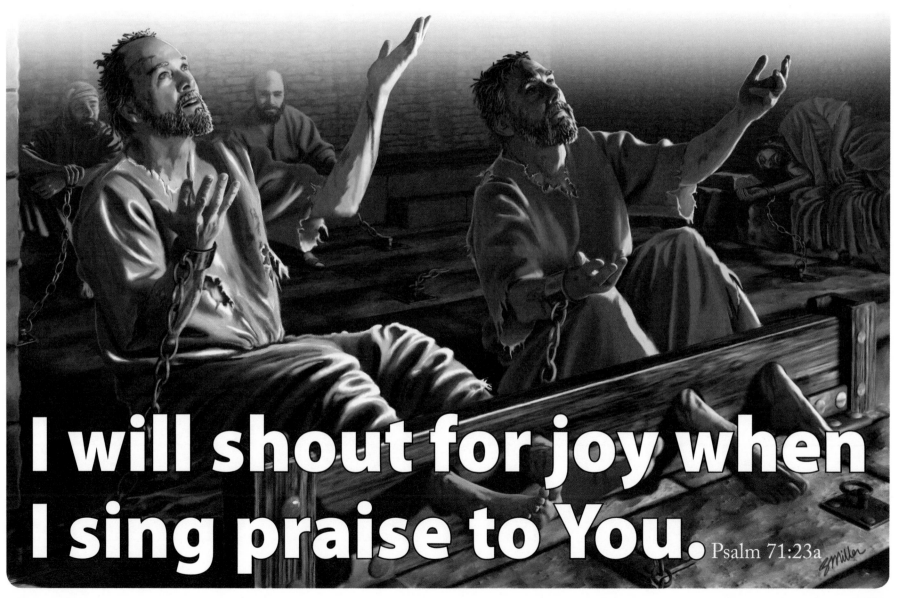

I will shout for joy when I sing praise to You. Psalm 71:23a

Paul and Silas were joyful in prison. Talk about the pictures. How can you be joyful in the places shown?

going shopping

waiting in line

trying a new food

riding a long way

**Name**

Paul and Silas were good friends. How can you be a good friend? Draw a picture of yourself helping a friend.

Paul and Silas sang to praise God. What do you use to praise God? Name the instruments. Complete each ABA pattern.

© Bible Preschool